DAILY AFFIRMATIONS FOR MEN

"BEING THE BEST VERSION OF **YOU**, **YOU** CAN BE!"

A 31 DAY DEVOTION

Copyright © 2025 Jermaine O. Edwards

All rights Reserved.

Introduction

"When I was a child, I spake as a child, I understood as a child, I thought as a child: but when I became a man, I put away childish things." - 1 Corinthians 13:11

New Focus

Day 1

Affirmation: "I am focused and determined. I set clear goals and work diligently to achieve them. My mind is sharp, and I stay present in the moment, channeling my energy towards what truly matters. With unwavering focus, I turn my dreams into reality."

Scripture: "Let your eyes look straight ahead; fix your gaze directly before you. Give careful thought to the paths for your feet and be steadfast in all your ways." - Proverbs 4:25-26 (NIV)

This passage encourages us to remain focused and dedicated to our goals, keeping our attention on the path before us and being mindful of our actions.

Be Attentive

Day 2

Affirmation: "I am fully present and attentive in every moment. I actively listen and observe, ensuring that I understand and connect with those around me. My mind is clear and focused, allowing me to give my best attention to every task and interaction. With mindfulness and awareness, I embrace the richness of each experience."

Scripture: "Listen to advice and accept discipline, and at the end you will be counted among the wise." - Proverbs 19:20 (NIV)

This passage highlights the value of attentiveness to guidance and correction, which ultimately leads to wisdom.

Meditation

Day 3

Affirmation: "I find peace and tranquility in each moment of meditation. My mind is calm, my body is relaxed, and I am fully present. With each breath, I release tension and invite serenity. I embrace the stillness within and connect deeply with my inner self. Through meditation, I cultivate clarity, balance, and a sense of profound inner peace."

Scripture: "But his delight is in the law of the Lord, and on his law he meditates day and night." - Psalm 1:2 (NIV)

This passage highlights the value of meditating on God's word consistently, finding joy and wisdom through contemplation and reflection.

Gratitude

Day 4

Affirmation: "I am deeply grateful for the abundance in my life. I appreciate every blessing, big and small, and I acknowledge the beauty around me. My heart is filled with gratitude, and I attract even more wonderful experiences and opportunities into my life by focusing on the positives."

Scripture: "Give thanks to the Lord, for he is good; his love endures forever." - 1 Chronicles 16:34 (NIV)

This verse reminds us to be thankful for God's enduring love and goodness.

Courage

Day 5

Affirmation:""I am courageous and brave. I face challenges with strength and confidence, knowing that I have the resilience to overcome any obstacle. I embrace new opportunities and step out of my comfort zone, trusting in my abilities and the journey ahead."

Scripture: "Have I not commanded you? Be strong and courageous. Do not be afraid; do not be discouraged, for the Lord your God will be with you wherever you go." - Joshua 1:9 (NIV)

This verse encourages us to be strong and courageous, reminding us that we are never alone.

Growth

Day 6

Affirmation: "I embrace growth and change. I am continuously evolving and improving, learning from every experience. With an open mind and a willing heart, I welcome new opportunities for personal and professional development. Each day, I become a better version of myself."

Scripture: "But grow in the grace and knowledge of our Lord and Savior Jesus Christ. To him be glory both now and forever! Amen."
- 2 Peter 3:18 (NIV)

This verse encourages us to continually grow in our faith, grace, and understanding, leading to a more meaningful and fulfilling life.

Forgiveness

Day 7

Affirmation: "I am open to forgiveness, releasing any anger or resentment that holds me back. I understand that forgiveness is a gift I give to myself, allowing me to move forward with a lighter heart. I choose to forgive others and myself, embracing peace, compassion, and healing. With a forgiving spirit, I create space for love and growth in my life."

Scripture: "Be kind and compassionate to one another, forgiving each other, just as in Christ God forgave you." - Ephesians 4:32 (NIV)

This verse encourages us to practice kindness, compassion, and forgiveness, following the example set by Christ.

New Beginnings

Day 8

Affirmation: "I welcome new beginnings with an open heart and an eager mind. Each day is a fresh start, filled with endless possibilities. I release the past and embrace the present, knowing that every ending is a stepping stone to a new and exciting chapter in my life. I am ready to grow, learn, and thrive in this new journey."

Scripture: "Therefore, if anyone is in Christ, the new creation has come: The old has gone, the new is here!" - 2 Corinthians 5:17 (NIV)

This verse reminds us that through faith, we have the opportunity for renewal and transformation, leaving the past behind and embracing a new beginning.

Purpose
Day 9

Affirmation: "I live each day with purpose and intention. I am aligned with my true calling, and my actions reflect my deepest values and passions. I trust that I am on the right path, and I am dedicated to making a positive impact in the world. With clarity and determination, I pursue my goals and fulfill my purpose with joy and gratitude."

Scripture: "For I know the plans I have for you," declares the Lord, "plans to prosper you and not to harm you, plans to give you hope and a future." - Jeremiah 29:11 (NIV)

This verse reminds us that God has a purposeful plan for each of us, filled with hope and a promising future.

Positivity
Day 10

Affirmation: "I radiate positivity and optimism. I choose to focus on the good in every situation, and I attract positive energy into my life. My mind is filled with thoughts of gratitude and joy, and I spread happiness to those around me. With a positive mindset, I create a fulfilling and joyful life."

Scripture: "A cheerful heart is good medicine, but a crushed spirit dries up the bones." - Proverbs 17:22 (NIV)

This verse highlights the importance of maintaining a positive and cheerful attitude, which can bring healing and strength to our lives.

Wisdom

Day 11

Affirmation: "I am wise and discerning. I trust my intuition and make thoughtful decisions. I seek knowledge and understanding, and I learn from every experience. With wisdom, I navigate life's challenges with grace and insight, always striving to grow and improve."

Scripture: "For the Lord gives wisdom; from his mouth come knowledge and understanding." - Proverbs 2:6 (NIV)

This verse reminds us that true wisdom and understanding come from the Lord, and by seeking His guidance, we can gain knowledge and insight.

Determination

Day 12

Affirmation: "I am determined and persistent. I face challenges with unwavering resolve and never give up on my goals. With each step I take, I grow stronger and more capable. I am committed to my success and embrace every opportunity to overcome obstacles and achieve my dreams."

Scripture: "Therefore, my dear brothers and sisters, stand firm. Let nothing move you. Always give yourselves fully to the work of the Lord, because you know that your labor in the Lord is not in vain." - 1 Corinthians 15:58 (NIV)

This verse encourages us to remain steadfast and dedicated, knowing that our efforts and determination are meaningful and valuable.

Humility

Day 13

Affirmation: "I am humble and grounded. I recognize my strengths and my limitations, and I appreciate the contributions of others. I approach each day with a grateful heart and an open mind, always ready to learn and grow. With humility, I build meaningful relationships and create a positive impact in the world."

Scripture:"Humble yourselves before the Lord, and he will lift you up." - James 4:10 (NIV)

This verse reminds us that through humility, we can receive God's grace and be uplifted.

Integrity

Day 14

Affirmation: "I live with integrity and honesty. My actions align with my values, and I stay true to my principles. I make ethical decisions and take responsibility for my choices. With integrity, I build trust and respect in my relationships and create a positive impact in the world."

Scripture: The integrity of the upright guides them, but the unfaithful are destroyed by their duplicity." - Proverbs 11:3 (NIV)

This verse highlights how integrity leads to a righteous and stable life, while deceit can lead to downfall.

Love

Day 15

Affirmation: "I give and receive love freely and abundantly. My heart is open, and I attract loving and supportive relationships. I am surrounded by love, and my life is filled with kindness, compassion, and affection. I express love in all my actions, and I am grateful for the love that enriches my life."

Scripture: "Dear friends, let us love one another, for love comes from God. Everyone who loves has been born of God and knows God." - 1 John 4:7 (NIV)

This verse reminds us that love is fundamental to our faith and our connection to God.

Health

Day 16

Affirmation: "I am healthy, vibrant, and full of energy. I take care of my body, mind, and spirit, nourishing them with love and care. I make choices that support my well-being and vitality. Every day, I become stronger and more resilient, enjoying a life of health and wellness."

Scripture: "Dear friend, I pray that you may enjoy good health and that all may go well with you, even as your soul is getting along well." - 3 John 1:2 (NIV)

This verse conveys a heartfelt wish for overall well-being and health.

Success

Day 17

Affirmation: "I am destined for success. I set clear goals and take intentional actions to achieve them. I am confident in my abilities and trust that my hard work and dedication will lead to great accomplishments. I attract success and prosperity into my life, and I celebrate each victory with gratitude and joy."

Scripture: "Commit to the Lord whatever you do, and he will establish your plans." - Proverbs 16:3 (NIV)

This verse encourages us to dedicate our efforts to the Lord, trusting that He will guide us toward success and fulfillment.

Peace

Day 18

Affirmation: "I am at peace with myself and the world around me. My mind is calm, and my heart is at ease. I let go of stress and embrace tranquility. I create a serene environment and surround myself with positive energy. Inner peace is my natural state, and I carry it with me wherever I go."

Scripture: "Peace I leave with you; my peace I give you. I do not give to you as the world gives. Do not let your hearts be troubled and do not be afraid." - John 14:27 (NIV)

This verse reminds us of the peace that comes from faith, encouraging us to trust and not be afraid.

Resilience

Day 19

Affirmation: "I am strong, capable, and resilient. I face challenges with courage and determination, knowing that I can overcome any obstacle. With each setback, I grow stronger and more resourceful. I trust in my ability to persevere and thrive, no matter what comes my way."

Scripture: "Blessed is the one who perseveres under trial because, having stood the test, that person will receive the crown of life that the Lord has promised to those who love him." - James 1:12 (NIV)

This verse encourages us to remain resilient and steadfast in the face of challenges, knowing that perseverance leads to blessings and rewards.

Self-Love

Day 20

Affirmation: "I am worthy of love and respect, starting with myself. I embrace my unique qualities and celebrate my strengths. I treat myself with kindness and compassion, and I forgive myself for any mistakes. I honor my feelings and take care of my well-being. I am deserving of all the love and happiness that life has to offer."

Scripture: "For you created my inmost being; you knit me together in my mother's womb. I praise you because I am fearfully and wonderfully made; your works are wonderful, I know that full well." - Psalm 139:13-14 (NIV)

This verse reminds us that we are uniquely and wonderfully made, deserving of love and appreciation for who we are.

Creativity

Day 21

Affirmation: "I am a creative being, full of innovative ideas and boundless imagination. I embrace my unique perspective and express myself freely through my creative endeavors. I trust my intuition and allow my creativity to flow effortlessly. With every challenge, I find new and inventive solutions, and I bring my visions to life with passion and joy."

Scripture: "For we are God's handiwork, created in Christ Jesus to do good works, which God prepared in advance for us to do." - Ephesians 2:10 (NIV)

This verse reminds us that we are uniquely created with purpose, and our creative abilities are a reflection of God's handiwork.

Balance

Day 22

Affirmation: "I live a life of harmony and balance. I prioritize my well-being and make time for the things that matter most. I balance work and rest, productivity and relaxation, and I find joy in every moment. I listen to my body and mind, honoring my needs and creating a balanced, fulfilling life."

Scripture: "But everything should be done in a fitting and orderly way."
 - 1 Corinthians 14:40 (NIV)

This verse reminds us of the importance of maintaining balance and order in our lives, ensuring that everything we do is done thoughtfully and harmoniously.

Clarity

Day 23

Affirmation: "I am clear-headed and focused. I trust in my ability to see situations with precision and make informed decisions. I embrace clarity in my thoughts and actions, allowing me to navigate life with purpose and confidence. My mind is open, and I welcome insights that guide me toward my goals."

Scripture: "Trust in the Lord with all your heart and lean not on your own understanding; in all your ways submit to him, and he will make your paths straight." - Proverbs 3:5-6 (NIV)

This verse encourages us to trust in the Lord, seek His guidance, and find clarity and direction in our lives.

Abundance

Day 24

Affirmation: "I am a magnet for abundance and prosperity. I attract wealth, success, and opportunities into my life effortlessly. I am grateful for the blessings that surround me, and I open myself to receive even more. My life overflows with abundance, and I joyfully share my prosperity with others."

Scripture: "And my God will meet all your needs according to the riches of his glory in Christ Jesus." - Philippians 4:19 (NIV)

This verse reminds us of God's promise to provide for all our needs, reflecting His abundant grace and blessings.

Empathy

Day 25

Affirmation:"I am empathetic and compassionate. I listen with an open heart and seek to understand others' feelings and perspectives. I respond with kindness and support, creating a safe and nurturing environment for everyone. My empathy strengthens my connections and fosters a sense of unity and understanding in all my relationships."

Scripture:"Rejoice with those who rejoice; mourn with those who mourn."
- Romans 12:15 (NIV)

This verse encourages us to share in the emotions and experiences of others, demonstrating empathy and genuine care.

Motivation

Day 26

Affirmation: "I am driven and determined to achieve my goals. Every day, I take proactive steps toward my dreams with confidence and passion. I embrace challenges as opportunities to grow and succeed. My inner fire fuels my perseverance, and I accomplish great things with enthusiasm and dedication."

Scripture: "And let us not become weary in doing good, for at the proper time we will reap a harvest if we do not give up."
 - Galatians 6:9 (NIV)

This verse encourages us to stay motivated and continue doing good, trusting that our efforts will be rewarded in due time.

Strength

Day 27

Affirmation: "I am strong, resilient, and capable. I face challenges with courage and determination, knowing that I have the inner strength to overcome any obstacle. I draw upon my inner resources and the support of those around me. I rise above adversity, becoming stronger and wiser with each experience."

Scripture: "Have I not commanded you? Be strong and courageous. Do not be afraid; do not be discouraged, for the Lord your God will be with you wherever you go."
 - Joshua 1:9 (NIV)

This verse encourages us to be strong and courageous, reminding us that we are never alone, and God is always with us, providing strength and support.

Patience

Day 28

Affirmation: "I am patient and calm. I trust the timing of my life and embrace the journey with grace. I remain composed and centered in all situations, knowing that everything unfolds as it should. With patience, I handle challenges with ease and wait for the right opportunities to come my way."

Scripture: "But if we hope for what we do not yet have, we wait for it patiently." - Romans 8:25 (NIV)

This verse reminds us to have patience and hope, trusting that good things will come in due time.

Mindfulness

Day 29

Affirmation: "I am fully present in each moment. I embrace the here and now with open awareness and gratitude. I let go of distractions and tune into the beauty of life unfolding around me. With mindfulness, I find peace and clarity, and I respond to each experience with calm and intention."

Scripture: "Be still, and know that I am God." - Psalm 46:10 (NIV)

This verse reminds us to take moments of stillness, to be mindful, and to recognize the presence and guidance of God in our lives.

Confidence

Day 30

Affirmation: "I am confident and self-assured. I believe in my abilities and trust in my decisions. I present myself with poise and speak with clarity. I embrace challenges with a positive mindset, knowing that I am capable of achieving my goals. I radiate confidence and attract success into my life."

Scripture: "So do not throw away your confidence; it will be richly rewarded. You need to persevere so that when you have done the will of God, you will receive what he has promised." - Hebrews 10:35-36 (NIV)

This verse encourages us to maintain our confidence and trust in God's promises, knowing that perseverance will lead to rich rewards.

Joy

Day 31

Affirmation: "I am filled with joy and happiness. I find joy in the simple moments and cherish the beauty around me. My heart is light, and my spirit is lifted. I embrace positivity and spread joy to others, creating a ripple effect of happiness wherever I go. Joy is my natural state, and I welcome it into my life with open arms."

Scripture: "The joy of the Lord is your strength." - Nehemiah 8:10 (NIV)

This verse reminds us that finding joy in the Lord provides us with strength and resilience. It encourages us to seek joy in our spiritual life and trust in God's unwavering support.

Made in the USA
Columbia, SC
17 February 2025